WE BIRTH FREEDOM AT DAWN

VOLUME TWO

BOOKS BY JAIYA JOHN

We Birth Freedom at Dawn, Volumes One and Two
Dear Artist: A Love Letter
All These Rivers and You Chose Love
No Man Came
Fragrance After Rain
Freedom: Medicine Words for Your Brave
Revolution
Daughter Drink This Water
Calm: Inspiration for a Possible Life
Sincerity of Sunlight: A Book of Inspiration
Fresh Peace: Daily Blossoming of the Soul
Your Caring Heart: Renewal for Helping
Professionals and Systems
Clear Moon Tribe
The Day Jumoke Found His Name
Legendary: A Tribute to Those Who Honorably Serve
Devalued Children
Beautiful: A Poetic Celebration of Displaced
Children
Reflection Pond: Nurturing Wholeness in Displaced
Children
Habanero Love: A Poem of Sacred Passion
Father to Son: Ode to Black Boys
Lyric of Silence: A Poetic Telling of the Human Soul
Journey
Black Baby White Hands: A View from the Crib

WE BIRTH FREEDOM AT DAWN

VOLUME TWO

JAIYA JOHN

Soul Water Rising

CAMARILLO, CALIFORNIA

AUTHOR'S NOTE

If you have read my prior work, you know
that all of this is just a Love letter from the
Great Mystery to our earthly yearning souls.
As such, with these two new volumes of
poems, stories, essays, prayers, and
devotions, I desire that you feel the intimacy
and urgency of where you and I now find
ourselves. Since late 2023, as horrific
massacre, new and old, slow and swift, in
many forms and lands, has at last captured
our collective human attention, our pain and
grief and resurgent Love have gushed through
my heart and being night and day. Like many
of you, my every cell and molecule has been
both decimated and revived. I have given
myself to this, our profound upheaval. I have
crumbled our heartbreak into the sea of this
unbearable season, this ongoing sermon of
sorrow and solace. In these soul waters, I
have soaked up our manna and nectar to
bring home to you.

These two volumes are the entire balm I have
been able to gather for you. *We Birth
Freedom at Dawn* is a book and birth water.
The title came to me as I ran up a steep hill on
a recent summer morning, sun blessing my
skin, sweat baptizing my ascendant birthing

time to push and deliver. Our ancestors have been with me in a hushed and cradling way during these months of mourning and morning. As this title came to me, Sojourner Truth and Harriet Tubman in particular settled in my bones and blood and breath. These two sturdy grandmothers have wet eyes as they hold us now. It is their insistence that we be free of our oppressive ways that has ushered forth these tribal words.

Sojourner and Harriet... Have you ever seen two monarch butterfly mates dancing in sunlight? They may to our eyes seem incredibly light of wing. Their flight, though, is a consequence of unimaginable struggle and endurance. And yet, here they are, still dancing, still joyful, filled with the orange of sun, bringing forth their generations.

This title, *We Birth Freedom at Dawn*, is what its offering is: A radical call. An invocation. A summons. To stir and galvanize and mobilize us. The word *We* is for our collective humanity. *Birth* speaks to our unconquerable Divine Feminine and its reclaimed role as we go forward, for the conception, gestation, and birth labor. For we already have this freedom. We do not have to chase it down. We have only to bring forth what is already in us and of us. The word *Freedom*: An acknowledgement of my life's work and ministry, including my earlier and kindred book *Freedom: Medicine Words for Your Brave Revolution*. And *Dawn*, a hopeful word, for our freedom soon come. It is not long now, dear soul. Not long. Our dark night of the soul too has its end.

This title is a declaration and decree. A promise and prophecy. An awakening and activation. A chant, hum, ceremony, remembrance song. To speak and feel this title is to call forth this freedom alive within each of us. Our freedom is stirring, nascent, divine, and truth. Soon, the fawning sprout begets the forest, and the raindrop begets the river. I pray these words bring back from the brink the many who are on the edge of despair, fear, hopelessness, terror, and fatigue. To allow us to see and feel and be what is coming and indeed what has always been here in the fertile earth of our sacred architecture. My God, these words are prayer.

WE BIRTH FREEDOM AT DAWN

AKAMU: LEGEND OF A SEA TURTLE

In the time when oceans ruled the world, and a heavy mist settled over land, a most amazing miracle happened. A sea turtle named Akamu was shaped into being by Sky God, who used Earth itself as Akamu's formation clay. Akamu experienced a mysterious birth. Her eggshell was made of hibiscus petals, which she shed at birth and then consumed as her first meal. This gave her unusual strength and beauty, and a sweet fragrance that announced her presence everywhere she went.

At birth, Akamu, like all hatchlings, made her way for the safety and home of ocean. When she first tasted sea water, a great wave rose up over her, and crashed down, scattering her and her sibling hatchlings. Akamu was tossed in the frothing tide. She became disoriented. When she gained her senses, her siblings were nowhere to be found. Akamu had lost her 'ohana, her family.

Akamu spent her childhood feeling lost in a world where no one looked like her, swam like her, or acted like her. She felt abandoned. Forgotten. Alone. As Akamu first began to mature into adulthood, her shell took on the splendor of hibiscus colors. Now and then, she would encounter *Honu*, other sea turtles. Their shells were sea green or sandy brown. Hers was a liquid swirl of bright yellows, pinks, reds, and oranges. She stood out visually. Other Honu noticed that Akamu did not travel with her own 'ohana. Akamu knew they noticed. She burrowed her head deep in her shell in shame. She longed for her siblings, for her parents, for her own Honu tribe. But she pained even more that other sea people didn't understand her. Couldn't relate to her ocean journey.

One fateful day, Akamu swam out beyond the far coral reef of a lush island. She dived down into a sea valley forested with kelp. She followed the valley deeper, until little sunlight reached the valley floor. She met a wise octopus who shared with her stories about the mystic purpose of 'ohana, solitude, belonging, and knowing your true self. The octopus introduced Akamu to a squid, a blue whale, a porpoise, and a clan of sea horses grazing the kelp. Each of these sea people shared with Akamu what they had learned about Loving yourself. It was in these moments that Akamu for the first time realized that her journey apart from her 'ohana was a gift from Sky God, an intentional path given to her so that she could learn parts of her soul she would otherwise never reach.

Akamu realized that the things that made her different were sacred medicine she was meant to share, with herself first, joyfully. And with the ocean world. Akamu realized this, and as she did, something like the sun rose in her heart. A tremendous light began to glow from inside her, illuminating the deep valley. Akamu's shell glowed, its colors a hypnotic dance of vibrancy. Akamu rose from the deep valley to the ocean surface. She swam for shore, where she burrowed in the warm sand. Legend has it that Akamu somehow miraculously birthed a whole new 'ohana of Honu. A special Honu who can only be seen when one's heart and soul are full of Aloha, full of Love. It is also said that Akamu's spirit lives in the white clouds and blue skies, comforting all souls who feel alone. And when

.14.

rain blesses the day, Akamu's glowing shell
can be seen.

Some call it a rainbow.

How big is your Love? Is it big enough to
break free from silence and inaction? We are
praying so. If it is genuinely Love, then it is
infinite and holds every soul in its care.
Injustice is a virus that thrives on shadows,
silence, and inaction. Call it out. Act. Drag it
into the light. Let this be how we redefine
what it means to live a successful life. If those
who would oppress and enslave are not
threatened by your existence, what does this
say about your existence, dear soul? Silence.
Passivity. Complacency. Complicity. A caste
system's best friends. Silence seems like a
good cave to hide in. Until you realize the
whole mountain is collapsing and your silence
is causing the avalanche. Chew off your
muzzle. Find your fierce song and fill the sky
with it.

Learning how to actively care for all people, regardless of their adjacency to you, can be challenging when you have been conditioned to care for only some people. A whole heart requires more vulnerability than a partitioned heart. And yet, with your heart wide open, you get to taste things you never did before. Like your pure, organic intolerance for oppression anywhere. The raw, exposed discomfort you may be feeling is the sensation of your shackles falling away. The chains that enslaved you to the global caste system are heavy. Maybe now you feel lightheaded, drifting, surreal. This is just a symptom of collective freedom infiltrating your brain and bones. Get used to the levitation that is the kindred liberation of souls.

Notice how those who advocate for the continuation of oppression are more hateful and violent than those who advocate for the end of oppression. Upholding what is unnatural is a desperate occupation, a monster making enterprise. Notice how campaigns to maintain oppression are fueled by hate, while campaigns to end oppression are fueled by Love. Behold this truth and ponder the contagious spiritual nature of our human arrangements.

Blessed Morning. I am honored to join you again today as we end this global colonizer project, this plague of centuries, violent blight on the sacred. Some of us are terribly addicted to colonizer culture. The separation pain will be immense. Nothing is more immense than the suffering this way of life has created. So let us die our necessary detachment. Land back to the people. All forms of land. In all lands. Everywhere.

They say that you speaking and acting against the violence of oppression is political. Oppression's violence is the most political behavior of all.

It is not true that you cannot save a single life
from where you are. Your personal acts of
rebellion against massacre are ripples that
bolster the tide of overwhelming global
sanction, the only force that causes tyrants to
halt.

.21.

Wake each day. Find the holy. Hold it close.
Let it speak and act for you. Renew your
collective liberation vows. Now is when you
root deeper into your holy things. Be a whole
ceremony unto yourself.

It should be the simplest, most natural thing in the world to want all souls free. Unless you don't.

Dear and Holy God, Great Spirit and Creator of all that is and may ever be. We bear forth our souls, kneel surrendered in Your soil, and, through our curtain of tears, we pray to You. We pray such piercing gratitude, that You have chosen our human family to walk this day's journey across the mystic bridge of generations, to endure the rampaging tides of epidemic, war, poverty, oppression. To receive these terrible tides, and gather them in spirit-baskets of Faith, Love, Compassion, and Devotion, bringing them to the sacred fire that crackles as it chants, *"We Shall Exist."*

We remember... the persistent nights, deep with despair and shackled in cold, through which ancestral mothers wept their souls, for their children's sake. And through which ancestral fathers cleaved their own hearts with knives purified in the flames, cleaved them open against the stars, so that night would bear witness to this sacrifice of self, for their children's sake. And the grandfathers and grandmothers, their eyes glistening in morning's revelry, would stretch their grieving bones and labored muscles, to uphold their duty, to live, to live until the River, until the Call to Light, live for our human family,

unspooling with every tenured breath the story
of our beginning, our midway, our horizon.
Stories, filled not only with the toll that troubled
waters bring, but also with the Greater Purpose
of our passage, the Intent soaked into floods of
crisis, that only those chosen for such ritual
scarification are called to bear.

We pray, Holy Redeemer, Sky of Glory, for
understanding: That we are not cursed with
these sufferings, rather that we are blessed and
released. Found and revealed. Carved, as an
indistinct boulder is shaped into masterpiece by
the unknowable inspiration poured through its
sculptor. That we see the hands of Grace moving
over our soul's terrain, plowing infinite acres,
crowning the high places, blessing the valleys
with surmountable sun, filling our river beds
with precious water, endowing our orchards
with fruits of resilience, weeding our pastures,
and flowering our meadows, steadily, Perfectly,
forging us in the intense mouth of circumstance,
bringing us ever into being, into its singular
resonance of *being human*.

And we dance. We dance for the music You
have sewn into the symphony of our expedition.

Our character braided and locked with the harmony that struggle brings, between physical existence and spiritual essence. With the melody infused into a people by common struggle, which though it may in our personal affliction seem so private and solitary, is by nature a bonding agent, even as the world sleeps through its deadlier affliction of forgetting its Holy Identity. And so, we course, like aged rivers, gathered of Grace and forward flowing, catching sediment from our banks in our immeasurable current, swallowing up our forgetfulness in waves of remembering. Thank You... for returning us to ourselves. Thank You... for revealing our true face. For dispelling illusions with a firm wind. Blowing away our human mist of blindness in the way You touch us.

And we sing. We sing the notes You have taught us by virtue of our mercurial experience, our tremulous triumphs against a backdrop of Truth. We are a particular tribe. Mustered from a certain dust. Imbued with a passionate Light. Our joy shall never leave us, for we are not victims in this play. Oh, Breath of Love, how You have visited us. How You have stayed. We feast on

Hope. We harvest Promise. These crops are plentiful and abundant in our burgeoning ground, for You have given us their seed. Even as we remember what all this traveling is for, we anticipate, we intuit, we glimpse the first glimmer of a more pronounceable Peace, sprouting in our deepest soul, seeking our Eternal Sky. We pray, for our circle, for our people, for we are fire walkers, and the flames, they ladder to Heaven and break upon our moments, tidal waves, demanding that we be washed and stripped to nakedness so that we may be clothed in the Awesome weavings of Your Grace. We drink now from Your crafted rain, falling so potently within this human drought. Thank You. We feed from this drumming totality of pain and joy, for sacredness requires a belly full for the voyage. You bleed us empty. You break us into wholeness. We have seen the Light of Your Instrumental Activity. Our Weather has Its way. Please, make us. Receive us. We walk with You. And we... we pray everlasting, unsayable Gratefulness. Knowing that You walk with us. And that You have made our path, Perfectly. We pray this to thee. Oh, how we say, Amen.

Remember when you were a child, and you prayed that adults would just make the world safe? Now is your chance to help fulfill the prayer.

Morning pledge. I rise and eat the truth of the day. I gather 80 acres of sky to wrap around my uncertainties, a sacred blanket as I confront the slaughter and its diseased breath of malice. I make sure to chew the sweetgrass that unleashes my voice. There are always expected silences to violate. I recruit more faith into my soul, that action may pour from me like mountain spring. Others drink coffee. I drink the sediment of suffering. It strengthens me as it fires my compassion. A people are being obliterated, I say. Where? You ask. Everywhere, I say. Who can stop this? You ask. Everyone. Everyone.

My people have endured a supremacy plague
of two thousand seasons. Do not try to
convince the offspring of genocide that a
genocide is not a genocide. We know what
extinction campaigns sound like. They sound
like the violence of a billion lies exhorting
each other to keep birthing lies. I was orphan-
born. I know storm. I know oppression's awful
nightmare cost. I know the holy worth of
freedom.

Being human is an intimate participation in a ceremony of sacredness. You must show up to the fire and contribute your flame. Especially when violence threatens to put the fire out. And if no one has taught you sacredness, now is the time to learn its interwoven ways.

You cannot cage, enslave, and dehumanize a people without caging, enslaving, and dehumanizing your own people. This is the paradox of harm. And a starting point for healing.

The grief and trauma will be lasting. It will
ripple generations into a wailing waterfall.
Our devotion to absolute collective liberation
must be more lasting. Deeper. Our
compassion cause must be stronger than the
pain, so we can hold it, heal it, set it free.
Look closely. Though the threads of our
present blanket may be sorrow-soaked, they
are Love-bound and kindred. We are weaving
a new world together.

Some people in your life are wondering when
you will stop speaking and acting out against
the violence of oppression. May they still be
wondering as you take your last breath. May
you return as spirit and keep them
wondering. May you become sky, earth, sun,
and water and keep them wondering. May
you show up in their generations and keep
them wondering. May you keep them
wondering for eternity.

Infect the generations after you with a fierce
intolerance for anything that reeks of
dehumanization. Infuse it into their DNA.
How? By the way you live your life.

No labor is beneath us if it moves the soul
within us, serves the suffering around us, and
blesses the prayer sky above us.

Your every act of expression, if it is rooted in Love and a desire for all souls to be free, is an act of revolution and resistance to the violent world order of exploitation and caste. Your deep breath, a poem aloft from your heart, kindness to a stranger, your dare to say anything, do anything at all. These are your active offerings, your humble shaping of the clay of our human culture. You must esteem yourself enough to know that even a single tear from your intentional heart trembles the ocean of our shared existence.

Collective freedom is not a seasonal hobby
you undertake. Not a charitable donation,
vacation, tourism, or trend. It is your way of
life. A dedication. Devotion. Decision to be a
perpetual ceremony that heals the whole of
us. Do you wish to be a helpful strand in the
sacred web of life? Every single day you must
exhume the conditioning buried in you, pile it
in the yard, and burn it away. You must
become a living chant, incantation, spell,
potion, formula that purges yourself and
those around you. It is not enough to be
healing. You must become that which heals.

Some will claim to be there for you, to be your mate, your kin, but then, when you are in dire need, they are nowhere to be seen. Maybe they were using you all along. Some use the word Love as a ruse, a strategy to get close to you and extract what they want. It can also feel like this when you and your people are being massacred, slowly or all at once. It can feel like the cruelest abandonment, an impossible betrayal, an aloneness unbearable to the soul. As though the universe and all its stars turned their backs on you and shunned you into oblivion. This is why, when a people are being killed, slowly or all at once, you must do everything you can so that they feel your soul, your Love, your very life fighting for their very lives. This is what it means to be present in the lonely rubble.

Maybe, one day, you too will be praying, with
every desperation of your soul, that the
whole world will come running to help you
and your people. Can you feel the feeling of a
prayer like this? Let it live in your heart, a
pure flower of mercy.

One of the healthiest, most liberating choices you can make is to not worship your government as your god. To not assume of your government morality, ethics, integrity, honesty, truth, or devotion. For, who is your government but an assembly of imperfect humans, each with their own assortment of fears, insecurities, agendas, motives, deceptions, ambitions, addictions, seductions, confusions, and self-betrayals. In the critical moments, which is every moment, when you must decide whether or how to respond to human horror and harm, seek not worship of your government. Seek the holy compass and divine government of your collective, ancestral soul.

Suffering is how Love cries out to itself in the world. You say you are Love. Will you answer?

Perhaps your greatest challenge each day is
not to stand up against the forces of
oppression, but to resist the ever-encroaching
tendency to feel that you are too small to
stop the forces of oppression. Remember, if
your soul and its actions are sourced from
Love and from your ancestors of kindred
spirit, not only are you not small, but you are
also immense infinity. When you are rooted in
the sanctity of collective life and liberation,
your soul size is legendary.

A revolutionary does not worship the way
things are or the way things have been. A
revolutionary does not believe in the god of
status quo, tradition, habit, beliefs, myths,
and norms. A revolutionary lives in the
visionscape of what is possible, even if the
possible seems impossible. A revolutionary
makes camp there, keeps fire there, and
forever ponders and reaches for the starry
night sky of miracles that ought to be.

Many people are uncomfortable with prophets and revolutionaries while they are alive, because those people do not want to admit that they are deeply attached to the way of life prophets and revolutionaries threaten. Our human challenge is not a moral challenge. It is a challenge to find the reason, the will, and the endurance to achieve change.

.45.

Another day. Another chance to end systems
of violence and remember sacredness. Arise
into your new day the way sun does. Do not
be timid and swept along in the mass fever of
violence. Pay close attention to who Loves
and cares for the land, and who destroys it.
You will know the source of the pain. And the
source of the medicine.

Violent organisms can only imagine violence
being done to them. They are self-fulfilling
prophecies that cannot fathom coexistence.
They are the root terror that projects onto
the entire world terrorist intent. If you want
to know their nature, listen to what they call
those who do not support their harm. They
are telling you their own composition.

.47.

Fear of annihilation is real for oppressed peoples. Oppressors appropriate this fear as their own, to win global validation for their annihilating ways. For oppressors, safety and security are code words for: *Let us kill*. Learn the playbook.

You have been conditioned your whole life to
believe that your vote is all that matters so
you will not realize that your voice (action)
matters even more. Your voice, when joined
by a chorus of millions, can create the
magnificent force needed to break a global
system of violence and resuscitate the human
soul.

We will not segregate our hearts so that you can continue enjoying this violent global system of supremacy and exploitation. We do not care whose status quo addictions must be rudely interrupted. We do not care whose caste traditions must be offended. The arrangements you have made with murder are not ours to keep. You may keep factory-producing villains and demons to justify your villainous, demonic project. We will continue illuminating and celebrating the sacredness and beauty of the humans you desperately need us to believe are not human. We will not fail to Love with Godly, borderless Love. We will not sacrifice our souls to the haunted canyon of hungry ghosts. We are devoted to healing our human beingness. We are determined to birth a new world. We will not segregate our hearts. Our tide is insurmountable. We swallow your sandcastles. We are life's ceremony of beauty. We will never stop dancing, singing, weaving, dreaming, praying, being, growing, gathering Grace.

As an aspect of Loving, if we are not
mourning each morning, we are not actually
all the way alive. Do not let distraction
console you. Your heart is big enough for
grief. Cherish your graces. And in your soul,
attend the burials of beautiful human beings
clutched away by monstrosity. Sing for them.
And forever after, do the daily labor of making
your soul inhospitable to apathy. Dig deep.
Assign rebel missions for your feelings.
Tourniquet your loss of courage. Instead,
bleed the sacrament that is your life.

When the earth shakes and the homes
crumble, or the water is poisoned, or the land
thieved, or the voices silenced, or the justice
violated, or the bombs fall, or the floods
come, or the fires rage, or the apartheid
reigns, or the bodies are noosed, or the
beauty is bleached, or the girls are stolen, or
the boys slaughtered, or the masses
murdered, or the vulnerable starved, or the
families un-nationed, and you do not in fact
care, because they are not *your people*, the
right kind of people, we who are still a soulful
kind of human, pray a merciful lightning will
strike your calcified heart and shock you into
the glaring truth-life that if we, for you, are
not your people, then in the ultimate realm of
spirit and Love, you are no one, nothing,
nowhere at all. Be not this. Be everything.
Examine what blocks your heart from feeling
and acting when certain groups are in crisis.
Dissolve this blockage, and you save your
own people. For, their time in crisis too will
come, and your open heart now will be a
prayer for hearts to open then. This is the law
of the sacred web of life. Indigenous ways.
Prayers up and actions ignited for all souls
and communities in crisis. Care is not a

feeling. Care is an action. Care acts. Caring is creativity with a cause.

*First published in *Dear Artist: a Love Letter*.

Do not leave the fire now. It has never been colder. Your flame has never been more necessary. Burn with us.

Fall in Love with those who have long been dehumanized. It is your Love that allows you to see their beauty, worth, and sacredness. It is your seeing that sets you free from your conditioned, dehumanized inaction. You must Love, so that you are willing to risk, sacrifice, and struggle. You must Love if you want to create the human condition that will one day save your people, too.

.55.

Do not argue with the infected. They are
infected, not unpersuaded. Instead, disinfect
yourself of supremacy virus, for it is
everywhere. Bolster your immune system
with daily ceremonies, gatherings with kin,
and organic Love recipes for prayers, feasting,
and necessary rebellions.

Those for whom group extinction is an obsessive science must be overpowered by those for whom collective well-being is a holy consummation. Oh, how you must burn for freedom.

WE CHANGE THIS WORLD

Every living soul is a world changer. We mock the idea that one person can change the world. And yet, the world is not a fixed object, chipped away at by a few special souls. Our world instead is a fluid element, continually ebbing and transforming in response to the force and nature of its every particle. The idea that one person cannot change the world is a virus disseminated and passed down by those who are infected with its docility code.

We affect our realm through the rippling, cumulative, exponential aura of our being. Delusion says our waves of action and energy stop at those who immediately encounter us. Laws of science and spirit say otherwise. A single smile of ours is a phenomenal comet, permeating social webs and physical distance as a persistent reverberation in the souls of humankind. In that these souls are ultimately a single soul (a sole soul) blossoming in Providential multitude, we therefore individually possess the power to touch the collective human heart in every moment of our existence.

Love and hatred are energy beams we emit
more constantly than breath. One beam,
purified. The other beam, polluted. We are
light emitting diodes. Depending on the
activation of our spiritual, emotional, mental,
and bodily circuitry, our light varies along a
spectrum of illumination on one end, and
cataract and myopia on the other. Seeing and
blindness. In our Loving moments, we
become sunlight for the mind and heart
flower of others, who then pass on and store
that expanding quality. In our bitter moments,
our pores exude an essence that insults the
sanctity and bruises the tenderness of
humans in their being.

Through our ideas alone we seed the soil of
our human imagination, dreaming, and
daring. Our tongues spread poison clouds or
healing mist, through even a single word or
briefest tone. At the very instance that we
crouch small in fearful self-doubt, we are
giants, stomping vulnerable populations in
our foul spirit, or lifting up entire generations
into Hope's atmosphere in our gigantic palm
of Faith.

We are not incapable. We are incredible. We do not live out our lives in the vacuum of consequence that our mind conceives. We are profoundly immersed in every life, in every tribe and lineage, throughout all epochs and eras. When the human thread trembles and holds in the gust, we are the fiber whose tensile strength is tested. We are the wind in the valley, rustling every leaf. We each are a clear crystal drop in a callous and caring stream, our brilliance and obstruction reflecting the total qualities of this earthly stream. To know a world, look inside its beings. To know a human being, look upon the world.

We are a created thing and so we carry creator gifts in our makeup. We are forever able, for we are the offspring of absolute Ableness. We must not fable this. It is Truth, an imperishable meal to be feasted.

Who among us dares to change this world? No dare is needed. We exist in this world, and so we change it.

Go in your heart and spirit to where the dying
is. Lie there on the same ground as them.
Stare up at the same sky as them. Feel and
see and hear and taste what they do.
Whatever passes through you, let that change
you forever.

There is a privileged palace in the soul where genocide begins. The conception begins with an inner voice that says: *Those people must be something horrible to deserve to be massacred like this.*

At one time, in every instance of devastating oppression and genocide, liberation seemed impossible. Oppressive systems seem invincible, right up until they don't. They are their most violent and blustering just before they are ended. This freedom work is a work of faith. You must believe, and imagine, a people free, to elicit your fullest sacred power and holy tantrum. Each day, each moment, find ways to renew your faith. If you must wail or chant or drum or quest or pray or sing or gather or wander the wilderness or purge your being or bathe in the belly of your passions, then do what you must. Doubt will mock you. Fear will rock you. Stay in your faith. Remember, you are not just a person. You are a people. Not some of them. All of them. Believe in your power.

This, right here, right now, is the revolution of
our time. If you are waiting for a more
convenient one, you are going to miss the
only one. Revolutions are never convenient.
They come with mourning. Are thrust upon
us. We do not choose them like vacations or
homes. They choose us. Do not wait for
history to tell you what to do. It will be too
late. History is always easier and less
accountable than the present moment. Like
now. Whatever you dream of doing on
the urgent behalf of humanity, do it now.

In many ways, it was your belief system that raised you. You inherited its way of being and seeing and feeling. Now that you are not a child, it may be time for you to raze your belief system. To crumble it to dirt so that you may raise it up as the garden of your own divine discernment. This is the only way for you to be medicine in this world, and not another perpetrator of harm rooted in generational lies and myths. You have the power and duty to examine the ideas collected in you and filter out what is toxic and oppressive. Make sure you do not keep any beliefs that may be seeds for dehumanizing any people. For, such seeds, if they remain, are the private beginning of very public, very massive harm. Politicians, governments, and corporations do not rule this world. Our personal and collective beliefs do. Here, in this contagious soil, is where we must work.

If the thought of an ethnic group of people
does not inspire in your heart feelings of
Love, beauty, brilliance, family, culture, art,
heritage, community, and kindness, as it
should when you imagine any people, then,
BeLoved, the groundwork for a particular
genocide was long ago laid in you, as it was in
so many. Do not feel shame. Feel inspired to
do the inner work to let Love's soul water
flow freely again in you.

May you gather even the most petite mercies
and miracles to sustain and embolden you.
For, this life is a collective river of pains and
pleasures, decided by each soul in each
moment. This is no game. You are no player.
You are no more or less than prayer.

A most spiritual act is to dissolve yourself in
the oneness of life, which means that when
others are suffering, you respond as though
you are suffering, because, interdependently,
you are. It also means that you work for
collective conditions that prevent suffering.
Spirituality is not a practice in comfort. It is a
practice in truth and action. A behavioral
manifestation of Love. And there is this:
Standing up against that which causes
suffering is spirituality unleashed.

Dear Creator. Grant us the strength to be all
the way present for this, and to let it break us.
Break us of our conditioned cages. Break us of
fear and comfort and conformity. Strike us
with your divine pain. Split and blacken the
trunk of our human tree. Life will find its way
through our charcoaled grief. Beauty will
grow again. And it shall be free.

All living things are alchemists, changing
energy into a kind of life. Our human anguish
is immense. So is your ability to garden
something kind and Loving with your
heartbreak and sorrow. You are a sponge in a
sea of everything. Your chemistry is endless.
You can give us your pollen of peace and pour
your resurrected empathy. Maybe your
delusions of equal opportunity have been
shattered on the rocks of reality. Gather the
shards and fashion a sculpture with your life.
Something the children might behold and call
Goodness.

Love's greatest act is not to comfort suffering,
but to treat the roots of suffering so that
suffering does not return. We must care more
to identify and heal our pathologies than we
care to avoid uncomfortable and pain
reckoning. To achieve this priority, we need to
address our attachments to systemic power.
Do not abandon the dying. Abandon your
allegiance to those who do the killing.

.71.

May you be ever so still inside. It is critical
now that you be in your highest discernment.
You must see everything for what it is and
what it is not. Be not the naive and gullible
child. Be the mother wading with her children
through a sea of souls and stories. Use your
holiest instinct and intuition. Pierce the veil of
social persuasion. Bear what this agony does
in your chest. It will show you what to do. Not
just now. For the rest of your life.

Not an atom, molecule, or cell inside you
does not wail with grief. This is how you know
you are still human. The world is not ending.
Our long sleep is. Now we stand sentry in this
sacred garden of souls. Only union allowed.
Your grief is a seed. Your action is the orchard.

At last, we see. Spirituality is an honesty.
Even about the horrific. Especially that.

This struggle is not genetic. It is kinetic. Not
between groups but between collective
spirits. Care for your energy, your spirit, your
soul. It is your inner condition that makes
a massacre or majesty of our outer world.

Let us pray that humanity matures to realize
that suffering is not a competition. If we heal
the roots of suffering in one people, we are
touching and healing the roots of suffering in
all people. When one people are mentioned,
it is not required that every people be
mentioned. We are not handing out ice cream
to children at a park. No one is being left out
when we sincerely address the human soul
and its sickness and glory. Everything touches
everything.

If your self-defense requires obliterating entire peoples, you need to examine what it truly is you are defending. Your supremacy system or your society.

BeLoved souls of martyred land. We feel your
breath. We feel sky shaking in your chest.
Olive trees crying. Melons bursting. Dirt in
your thirsting. Your haunting hunger. Your
blood rushing to sea. Sea foam spitting. All
the kites grounded. Your song persisting.
Children shocked forever. Children taken.
Fathers taken. Sisters taken. So much
forsaken. Not enough bread. Rare bites of
rice. Families made spirit. Memories stuck on
power lines. Bruised vines. Orphaned dreams.
Impossible screams. So many salted streams.
Silence. Sometimes foreboding. Sometimes
reprieve. Prayer call, still. Prayer call gushing.
Tears tracking cheekbones. Tears rivering
blood, dust, dread. So many embraces. Last
letters. Last kisses. First kisses. Fast kisses.
Ache for what heart misses. Cold earth bed.
Cold mattresses. Walls made wind. Roof
made sky. Terror on prowl. Night's
uncertainty. Morning's dread. Another sun.
Another breath. Begging for help. No one
come. Stranger come. Kingdom come. Clarity.
Rarity of stillness. Whistle of death from sky.
Why. Why. Why. Worship. Plea. Warming fire.
Endless fire. Faces in the fire. Life on fire. So
tired. So scared. So alone. Home. Sudden loss.

changed forever. God. Angels. Drums.
Resistance. Child prophets. Lambs. Black
goats. Water nowhere. Food nowhere. Pain
inside. Pain outside. Still Love. Still kindness.
Still intimacy. Still mercy. Still life. Still life.
Revelation. Humanity. Pain. More pain. No
relief. Monsoon grief. Morning laced with
mourning. Culture cradling. Cold soup ladling.
A land. A language. A mystery answered.
Love. Children. Joy. Moons. Too soons. Too
late. Shards of hate. Crucifixion. Resurrection.
A people. Poetry. Persistence. Birth. Beauty.
Feast. Gathering. Freedom. Drum. Dance.
Searching. Finding. Horrified finding. Holding.
Rocking. Swaying. Seeing. A people. A land.
An earth. Rebirth. Life. Still life. Eternity.

Witness honestly, around the world and
throughout the times, who calls who terrorist.
And who behaves as one.

Imagine. No.... Feel. *Feel.* Everyone and everything you know and Love slaughtered. While the entire world argues about it.

Precious soul and life. It is so easy and so tempting to activate your primal brain and fall into the abyssal tar pit of *Us vs. Them* thinking. This is a death trap. It enlists your body, mind, spirit, emotions, and soul in a war of hostility, rigidity, narrowness, hardness, and ultimately violence. It also makes your perspective easier to invalidate and dismiss, as your perspective is rendered flat and one-dimensional in a world of richness and interweaving. You do not have to reduce and dehumanize yourself to contribute to revolution.

Genocide and oppression are not about choosing "teams," an attitude that insults the sacredness and gravity of people suffering and dying. This is no game. There are no teams. There is only suffering and dying. Honor this. Affiliate yourself with nothing less holy than liberation and freedom.

When you dig another people's grave with tools of violence, the grave becomes your own, not from vengeance, but because you inherit from your own harm the chilling, lonely emptiness of having lost your entire soul.

Behold the violent spirit that tries to erase a people but only succeeds in etching them more deeply into the heart of humanity. Be assured, oppression haunts the oppressor.

To be a bystander to atrocity is a kind of
slavery that makes your fears your master.
Inaction is a plantation that swallows the
spirit of your life. Go up on the mountaintop
and proclaim to the world the horror in the
valley. You may be alone, but the sky will hold
you and your soul will be fertile with the
breeze of integrity.

If you are terrified of speaking out, your terror is evidence that oppression exists. You don't have to see gravity to believe in it. Just feel it pressing on your bones and breath. Oppression presses, too.

Every soul is a refugee. A breath of Grace
away from aloneness, homelessness,
landlessness, lifelessness. Prayers up for those
under violent, genocidal assault worldwide.

In every precious moment of your life, spark, conceive, gestate, birth, and raise collective freedom. Live your life in a way that dissolves oppressive systems and heals the harm they have caused. Be divinely devoted. From this day forward the deepest root calling for each of us, regardless of our profession, must be collective freedom. We have no choice.

A LOVE CALCULUS

Multiply the number of groups of people you
hate by the number of individuals in those
groups. The sum equals the number of
reasons, causes, and triggers for you to
experience the feeling of hatred in your heart,
not only at those times of direct encounter
with those people, but also in each and every
moment of your life. Every one of those
moments is a fertile ground for you to think
about, imagine, and contend with those
people. Your life is literally a minefield you
walk, constantly stumbling over the mines of
hatred you have chosen to plant. You even
intentionally run to those mines and jump on
them, so great is your determination to hate.

You can never escape triggering the sensation
of hatred, which is not pleasurable but
instead is a sour current of misery and
suffering you channel through every particle,
cell, vessel, and organ of who you are. You
have chosen to inundate yourself with hatred,
a monsoon flood of never-ending ailment, all
because you have decided that you have good
reason to hate this group or that group. Your

true joy has become a limp, lifeless carcass,
drowned in the flood of your reasons to hate.

Some of us are passionate explorers of that
barren terrain yielding reasons to hate. We
expunge all awareness and memories of any
possible goodness in a people, any hint or
potential of worth or value, just so we can
hunt freely for hate-reasons. We want the
open-season without catch or kill limits.
Whenever we come upon a flare-up of
humanness, dimension, or texture in our idea
of a people, fear and discomfort strike us as
though we have encountered the beginnings
of a forest fire. In the flush of this unsettling
contradiction to what we seek—hatred-
worthy characteristics in others—we reach for
our water bucket of mental erasing and douse
the flame. We are here in this land, this place
of strategic reasoning, to discover artifacts
qualified for hating. We are not here to see
beauty or worth. We kill with volatility
whatever gets in the way of our expedition.

In the end, when you have multiplied the
reasons for your hatred by the population size
of your hated groups, you have unwittingly

painted yourself into a corner in which you cannot step, look, reach, breathe, think, or even feel without stumbling over a self-chosen reason for hatred. You have harvested hatred and because your mind is magnificent in its power, you have accumulated a vast and burdensome harvest.

Now imagine a different harvest. Summon the Love you have for someone you hold dear. Experience that feeling of warmth and bliss cascade through your being. You have now blessed and baptized yourself in the endless reservoir of Love that you have in you, all because you have decided you have good reason to Love this particular person. Now you are drowning in Love, your joy a vibrant light illuminating this flood.

Ask yourself: *Which feels better to my heart and soul? To hate or to Love?* If Love is your answer, you are fortunate, for you have the means to fill your life and vessel with that which feels good to your heart, mind, and soul. All you have to do now is make another decision: Choose to expand your Love. That which you feel for that special person, people, or group, simply break down your stingy walls of exclusion and extend your Love! By nature, Love will flow anywhere you allow it. Like water, it will fill, soak into, and become the essence of all that you let it touch. It is the Bright Monsoon. All you need do is choose to Love.

Decide you have good reason to Love that group, and that group, and that one. Go crazy admitting more and more groups into your house of Love, regardless of their imperfections or the way they discomfort or challenge you. Become a stubborn Lover even in the face of those who scorn you. Become a seer of your Love's roots in others. Become a graffiti artist with Love as your paint. Spray it over even the most desolate human souls. Beautify and resurrect them. Bring them to life. Your life of Love.

Eventually you will be able to calculate incredible mathematics. You will be able to multiply the number of groups you have chosen to Love by the number of individuals in those groups. If you decide to decimate all your walls and come up with reasons to let the whole world in, you will have blessed and baptized your entire life and every moment of your life. You will have blessed yourself with causes, reasons, and triggers for your heart, mind, and soul to be flooded with and experience the blissful sensation of Love. Not because the world came begging for your charity, its carts loaded with reasons for your Love, but because you chose to come up with your own reasons. Because you wanted to have endless triggers for your stream of moments in which you could not help but constantly, in your movement, thoughts, and imagination run into human reasons to let loose your Love. Make this choice and you will have solved the greatest calculus of them all.

Supremacy is making its final stand.
It will fall.

Our group identities in some ways are killing
us. If you. Or I. Choose a group. And then get
to intimately know each member of that
group. We will find that each soul is unique.
Each soul dreams the group differently. The
idea of this group does not hold water. The
group is an illusion. A delusion. If you get to
know a single soul from a group, the group
dissolves. It disappears. Friend, we are living
our whole lives allegiant to, killing on behalf
of, dying for, a thing that does not exist.
Except as an idea in the being of souls who
are very real. Maybe what we really want are
not group identities, but relationships. A
fertile land that bears fruit and is kind to us
and Loves us organically without additives.
Relationships. These, too, are so very real.

You cannot fool a people who have been
oppressed for centuries. We know oppression
when we see it. We can feel it, hear it, smell
it. It has an undeniable stench. You can tell us
it is not oppression, that it is clean,
wholesome, righteous. But your words mean
nothing because your odor is profoundly
murderous. We know you. We know your
ways. No costume you wear can deceive us.
We have gained freedom eyes.

CALMING THE TIDE

Our world is inflamed. Chronic inflammation becomes disease and death. These are the laws of not only the human body but also of the collective organism that is humankind. Even the tide needs to rest. Even the shore needs respite from the battering of the tide. And where then does human well-being reside? In the calming of the tide.

We were given anger as a trigger for the flood of adrenaline through our system in precise, acute instances when our survival is threatened. Anger is a useful tool in certain concentrated moments. But our rage has grown so unabated and relentless that it has paralyzed in the release position the valve that would contain it. The floodgates are stuck open. Social change has often visited us in periods of years, pronounced of fury and frustration. Perhaps our current season is but the build up toward an explosive thrust forward. But this does not feel like anger born on the wings of justice and dignity. It feels more like an anger brewed in the fester of self-destruction. It does not appear to be leading us to emancipation or liberation but simply toward more anger.

Chronic inflammation causes disease and death because all of life is designed to exist in a state of balance, whether within organisms or between organisms. Anger is not a state of balance but a state of excitement or exaggeration. It strains our natural systems and their capacities. It scars the arteries and organs of our individual bodies and does the same to the unseen spirit-arteries that connect us in the social world. Chronic inflammation hardens arteries and hearts and exacts the same toll on societies. We lose compassion, patience, understanding, respect, regard, and the ability to communicate because we suffer a hardening of our cultural organism. Compassion requires pliability in order to flow just as arteries do to optimally channel the flow of what keeps us living. Our culture itself is losing its compassion as anger rages against its walls.

The way we treat each other is a reflection of how we treat our inner selves. How we regard each other tells a story about how we regard ourselves. If we are constantly attacking others with our anger, there must be a preceding act. We must have already been attacking our own internal being with that same anger—first the cup must fill itself before it overflows its boundaries and floods another.

Our own national leaders too often practice campaigns of spite and denigration against domestic "adversaries" and foreign "enemies", rather than practicing the art of communication; the transmission of ideas; and the crafting of harmony. Our cultural parents in this sense were scowling bullies. And what does this wrath gain the soul? Lacing our words and actions with the intent to cause hurt to others does not render their opinion mute or void; does not elevate our own opinion; does not make us superior; does not impress the wisdom of generations; does not ingratiate us to some mythical court where the titles of courage and righteousness are bestowed upon the most hurtful souls.

Our so-called *democracies* are often born not of a democratic process but of the violent supernova of war. As children of this violent birthing, we are responsible for reckoning with the violence that was born into us. This befalls especially our younger societies as we grow into national adulthoods. The tone and tenor into which we are born and raised seeps deeply into our marrow, is born again in the way we live out our days. Now our human children suffer from the generational amplitude of an angry cultural rain.

We absolutely denounce our youth for shooting each other over a pair of shoes, a fashionable jacket, or for neighborhood territory. But who are their models for this behavior? We are their models. We who fly into a rage when we suffer a perceived transgression while driving; we who imagine slaying the other driver with the dagger of an extended middle finger, our faces exploding into bright red pumpkins over the slightest traffic imposition; we of spit and fury who attack each other with fists and furniture on national television—all because we have been invited to make a spectacle of ourselves (what state of being is this when we would embarrass ourselves simply because we have

been invited?); we whose default mode for
solving any conflict or perceived threat is
hateful verbal assault and violence; we who
kill to show our children that killing is wrong.

We are the teacher, the mentor, the authority,
the preacher when it comes to our children
and their ways of relating to this world. Their
behavior is but a billion newborn spiders
bursting from the egg sack of our behavior.
Connections all around us—between our
inflammation and theirs—but we strain to see
the link because of our huff, bluster, and blur.
We are all wound up and spinning. We are
the hurricane. Hurricanes cannot see clearly
that which they destroy because they are too
busy spinning. The panorama in front of them
is truly blurred. There is no clarity of vision
while whipped into a storm of anger. We miss
the connections between ourselves and our
children. The connections appear to us as
spider webs—we only see them if the light
catches the webs just right; or if we race
through the web and it sticks to our face
(another child dies). Because we encounter
the connections in this uncomfortable way—
as a nuisance—we brush the connections

away, just as we brush the webs from our face. We are in too much of a hurry and in too much anger to spend time with connections and webs.

Our children are growing up angrier than we are. This escalation will continue until the boiling pot erupts and all things are destroyed. Then, in the sudden, chilling, silence of nothingness, we will finally pause to realize just how angry we all are. And that the growing roar of our yelling, screaming, stabbing, shooting, bombing, killing was not in fact a sign of progress but rather was a signpost along the way to our own demise.

When a family is suffering from the dysfunction within it, intervention has always been a tried and tested mode of resolve. We need now what elder cultures always turned to. As a societal family, we need an intervention. We need to gather around the circle and speak light onto what we have become, and speak life into our dreaming and walking of the healing path.

Transforming anger is a process that largely eludes our younger national cultures. But much older cultures bring us lessons of the possibility. There is a catch. For children to actually learn something from their grandparents, they must first sit still long enough to listen to the story. They will not sit in the first place if they do not respect their grandparents as having something meaningful to offer. Our young, colonial national cultures often struggle to respect such grandparent cultures enough to submit to them as teachers. But our stressed-soaked desperation has forced us now to turn more than ever in this direction for relief. This is a metaphor of cultural humility and opening ourselves up to the truth of our own dying.

If we realize our dying, is this enough to get us to stop running madly around the yard, and to finally stop and sit at the foot of our grandparent cultures? What they have to tell us involves transforming the energy of anger. Some people wish to label this concept New Age. Such an attitude is not only incorrect but completely the opposite of the truth. Transforming the energy of anger is a wisdom descended from the oldest ages of all. These ways of healing are not built upon self-centered relationships with external sources and pharmaceutical bandages. Their foundation is centered in the whole—the whole body of life and humanity of which we are a part. The mechanism and source are internal—of spirit, mind, and body. And the transforming process is constructed of good old-fashioned practice, practice, practice. These truths populate the core of most faiths. Whatever our religious or spiritual manner, we may incorporate the science and wisdom of transformation in such a way that our faith becomes *even more* effective and meaningful in our lives.

We need shepherds who will show us the way from the valleys of rage out into the meadows of compassion. When we perceive all around us to be menacing, who will teach us to recognize a smile? We need storytellers whose yarns and fables spill out truth that floods us and our children with daily milk of humanism: the art of existing in a way that nurtures humans *being*. But to stand for this today is to attract flame throwers who shriek that compassion is for weaker nations and wispier people. Everywhere we turn seeking peace, there is a flame thrower waiting to scald us back into anger, back in inflammation. We audition shyly even before our young for the role of peaceful models. But because we have not invested sufficiently in our internal transformation, the first flame thrown from the threatened anger-monger blows us back. We leave the stage having never fully become the character of peace.

And surely peace is a character. We must learn her motivations. We must rehearse her lines. We must forget our rash-erupted selves and dive completely into this new being, this shepherd that waits within us all. She is an elusive habit to which we must trek. She is a place so high we are required to scale her slopes until our blood runs. Transformation is not supposed to come in easily through the window. We must chase it. Repetition of certain thoughts and the un-learning of other thoughts will cause a wonderful morphing in our very consciousness. This change will open us up to our festering woundedness, from which feeds our roach-like prejudice. And what is prejudice but the act of molding anger and fear into a fireball for throwing at the monsters we believe chase us? All we manage to hit, for the most part, is people who happen to be in the way, people who have nothing to do with the monsters of our minds.

So now, who among us will be courageous enough to take internal steps forward toward changing the channel, transforming the frequency, calming the private clamor of inflammation? No pharmaceuticals exist for this. What ails the collective body human is what ails the personal body of human beings—an inflammation born of wounds unattended. There is a great healing to be done. This is the final frontier of our kind. Here, in the internal space that itself goes on forever, not out there in the external space beyond this Earth. There is this inner world, and that is all. And this world is ailing not of ideas and opinions but of a hostile wind. In this hostility our ideas and opinions become not seeds scattered for fertility, but daggers blown with hurricane force through human hearts.

Let us go about finding our shepherds, the ones who will teach us something of the calming of the tide. In the silence of daily contemplation is a promising hint about where we may find these sage guides. Old cultures whisper to us in every moment:

The shepherds live within.

Our human condition. Everywhere. This is much more than heartbreak. It is soulbreak. Someone sing a medicine song.

LOVE IS LIFE

Some believe that Love and hatred are equals.

Hatred is never satisfied. Love is born satisfied. Hatred when responded to with hatred only grows more hateful. When responded to with Love, hatred has only two options: It can grow more hateful, or it can transform into Love. As long as hatred remains hatred, it cannot be fulfilled. It is a raging calamity, lost in its own self-punitive vortex. It is a voracious ghost, starving but never being filled. For what it seeks— destruction—by nature is not filling but depleting of soul. The true hatred cultivators are vacuous of peace, for hatred has a singular nature: suffering.

Love, by nature, is born satisfied. When responded to with other Love, it can only bloom deeper into its field of contentment. When responded to with hatred, Love can only be sparked into a more compassionate Love. Only by allowing hatred to flare in response to hatred can a heart not be satisfied. But then that heart is not Love being unfulfilled. It has first yielded to hatred, and now is unfulfilled. As long as the heart is saturated in Love, that heart is fulfillment, is satisfaction.

Love is our essential DNA. Hatred is a virus. It can sicken Love's vessel, overtake it. But hatred cannot live without Love. Once the host, Love, dies, hatred too expires. For hatred must breed on something, in something. Hatred is dependent. It sucks from the teat of woundedness to feed its gruesome appetite. Its gnashing is futile, for it devours Love, a nutrient that cannot nourish hatred. Hatred is a maddened leech fastened to Love's tender belly. It will go where Love goes—always leeching, always lurking.

Love though can live without hatred, for Love is Life. It is Life's surging breath, that effusive element, that luminous pulsing. Shining so, it attracts all things, including hatred. Strong Love wilts that hate-weed, incinerating its foul design. Hatred is a bully on the yard. Love is the yard. Bullies are eventually exposed as farce. What is earth and true remains.

Hatred closes the heart like a suffering fist. Love opens the heart, a flower blossom undeniable. Love gives birth to life. Hatred gives birth to destruction. One is light, one steals light. Hatred fools itself into believing that domination will bring it peace. What it gets instead is a burning spear, soaked in hatred that wants to return home…. to hatred. In this way, hatred is a self-mutilator, a hacker of its own limbs. It spills its entrails on the rusted gate of its own enclosure. It is a closer. Of all that is open.

Love is Life. Hatred is a noxious cloud passing through the sky of Love. Love remains the sky before the cloud comes, while the cloud is present, and after the cloud passes. Love's sky is larger than hatred's cloud. It contains hatred's cloud, which can disappear, dissolve into Love. Love cannot be dissolved into hatred. It can only be eclipsed by hatred. Love is essential nature. Hatred is not of that essential DNA. It is an interloper, insidious, persistent, relentless. But it is not the nature of Life. It is the blemish on that nature. Some believe that Love and hatred are equals. Another truth speaks out: Love is Life. Hatred

is a shadow made noticeable only by the light
and life of Love. This eternal sun is our
baseline, our default, our original setting at
conception. This is how we began: in Love.

May we will stop worshipping governments as
our gods and begin to be accountable for the
world we desire.

Your voice carries thunderous spiritual power.
If you call out to those who are under horrific
assault, you must believe they will feel the
presence of your soul. Send yourself to them.
Speak. Act. Cry out your Love.

My God, fear has silenced us for ages while rabid men with deadly toys ejaculate their egos over beautiful lives and steal from living things the songs that freedom sings. But our heavenly song on earth is an irresistible revival. And feet will stomp and hearts will beat in the new and glorious morning.

Because I Love you, I have no choice but to care for you, my human garden. Our roots are woven down where eyes do not see. And the spring I want depends on the dying of your denial.

Mama, when will they stop killing us?

When someone stops them, my Love,
my sweet garden.

Oh, Holy Night. All the lands are weeping. The stars are a braille that's saying: *May Mercy be in your praying*. Oh, for a silent night. A bombless night. And all the children sleeping.

If you search the depths of your soul, you can always find something to offer to revive our freedom fire.

So many tears that the Sea of Galilee is rising.

Dear Creator, Holy Light, Precious Love. We thank you for your Mercy prior, now, and to come. We are lost. We wail our despair deep in a dense forest through a long, moonless night. Our way out feels impassable, yet you have already rendered the way. Too much blood water and tear water spills from us. We are drought and desiccation. You mend our severe serrations. You give us back our salty sea. For so long we have practiced violence as our salvation. It is our howling demise. You offer us the bread of a bold and beautiful way. We pray now for the appetite to eat your offering. Our children are soft seeds tossing in a tornado of terror. You have already prepared their gentle landing. Their miracle season of tenderness. Sky hurts to breathe. What are your endless stars saying? We want to sing their medicine. We thank you for the courage you grant us to pierce our paralysis. We thank you for allowing us to choose to be new.

What manner of being are we? This earth is our answer. Our aching testimony. Thank you, Infinite Eternal. For our wander. For our way home.

Love is fiercest when the harm is most
profound. May we continue to be devoted to
ending mass violence and oppression
worldwide, treating their roots, and standing
fiercely by those who suffer dehumanizing
pain. Though the dark night of the soul be
long and cold, freedom comes in the
mourning.

Grief is the oceanic ache of Love blooming into its purest flower. Grief is how Love lets go, so that Love may be made new. Grief, a weeping doorway to Love's purest form. A million Love poems birthed each day in the heart. If you channel grief divinely, you summon the power of Ages. A holy power that ends empires.

You do not stop the massacre of a people only
for those people. You stop it to stop the end
of everything. Whatever is most precious to
your soul is what is at stake when you resist
or submit to oppression anywhere.

The question is not: *Are you tame enough to be "civilized?"* It is: *Are you wild enough to be free?* Wild freedom from all forms of oppression everywhere. To stop genocide, you must be willing to sacrifice your lifelong ideas and your attachment to them. You must be willing to become unaffiliated in your soul. So that you can see. Seeing, you will feel. Feeling, you will activate your whole soul into this actual life.

Everything is a cycle, and the sea shall swell
and trough, and the tide shall rise and fall,
and the anointing shall pass its seasons. Your
calling will lead you through every emotion
and condition. Embrace this river. It will bring
you home.

Healing the disease that manifests as oppression and dehumanizing mass violence often requires swimming against the tide and upstream against a forceful current. But when you reach those mighty compassion waters, you and your kindred spawn a liberated way of life.

Imagine a world in which compassion and empathy for the suffering of others is held sacredly and above conquest and control. Be such a world inside your soul. For, you are the soul of this world. Care for your garden.

Who is teaching peace in the soul?
We should gather there.

There will always be those who are
determined to believe that no one is
oppressed, and that everyone exists in their
own earned station. This is the very essence
of supremacy and inferiority delusions. Be
careful that you are not infected. Forever
check the roots of your soul.

If you do not see the matrix,
you have become the matrix.

The most dangerous thing about genocide is
that people prefer not to believe it is
happening. It is this disbelief that fuels and
enables it. It is painfully difficult to accept
that humans, governments, and societies can
be capable of mass slaughter. The price of not
accept what is true before us is generational
trauma and devastation after us. If you are
trying to come up with reasons why
massacring a people may be necessary and
justified, you are already lost. As to what you
see with your very eyes…. If you cannot
decide, it's genocide.

Pray that your people never need the world to save them. Pray that we heal enough to save us all.

You get to live the rest of your life becoming sweet medicine for the world, if you choose. What a gift. Your soul is filtering the world's goodness and malice. Be clear as to which you want to let through.

Legal and social arguments about the intent of genocide are beside the point. If a people are being destroyed, they are being destroyed. Humanity is accountable. A house on fire burns regardless of intent. Those with a soul put out the fire. Our governments will not save us, for they have no soul. It is upon us to put out this fire.

It is time that we acknowledge the racist
origins and use of the term *terrorist* and begin
to also apply the term honestly and
accurately to those entities that use terror to
maintain oppressive power. When we remove
the racist iconography of *terrorism*, another
face is revealed. One that has been
historically promoted as goodness and
decency. We have no choice but to finally
demolish the infested, rotten house of
supremacist ideologies and build a human
home that is viable for collective life.

This earth is an intimate weaving. All regional violence is global violence. All global violence is also local. It is a fatal mistake for us to believe that a particular mass violence is regional. Mass violence anywhere grows from roots in spiritual sickness everywhere.
The horror can reach us, too. May our urgency and self-concern match this cold, inevitable truth. Indigenous ways see the interwoven web of life. This seeing sparks accountability for the whole. There are no foreign troubles. It is all intimately personal for us all.

Here is what we should know about *those people*. If you have a soul, all lands and people live within it, for the entire world lives in every soul. It is astounding how we complicate human coexistence. Which is precisely what is necessary for exploitation. Never lose touch with sacredness. It holds us whole. Root yourself dearly in empathy and compassion, so that the malice does not swallow you. We need your heart to remain beautiful. Bear witness. Hold the line.

The light. The shadow. The living thing. It is vital at this time that we be well enough to discern these three aspects of the mass violence erupting in so many other lands. These aspects reflect the intimate violence long festering in our souls. We need far more than just critical thinking. We need centered, stilled, and clarified spirits. We need spiritually rooted souls. We need to continuously tend to our bodies, to keep the pain moving through and out of us, so that grief does not make too terrible a home. Daily, we need to flush, purge, move, caress, and soothe our bodies and minds. They are foundations in our capacity to endure horror and still coexist beautifully. And we need to gather. In all the ways. Not only physically, but, more than anything, in spirit. Someone prepare the food. Someone pour manna from the moon. Someone settle the children. Someone, please God, someone stoke the freedom fire.

If a child can endure months, years of horror
and still fashion sweetness, we can behold
their reality and cradle their sorrow. Moons
are coming that we have not seen before. Let
us see if we find the will to make a softer
world with this new kind of moonlight.

BeLoved. Have you examined and softened your belief system today? Your lifelong conditioned beliefs may be harming you and ending all of us. But if you turn your belief system into a kind of air, a thing permeable to life and joy and suffering, it may help us to breathe like living things. And you may become not a rigid detonating bomb of ideology, but a sacred song that helps us heal.

I spirit walked through all the lands of
Levantine. It was divine. Unbroken souls
broke bread in Palestine. It was divine.
Goatherds, shepherds, poets, and physicians
held each other with a closeness only grief
can cause, as their hearts were so inclined. It
was divine. Widows weaving sang their tears
and pined and pined. It was divine. Children
ran, somehow still gleeful like summertime. It
was divine. Sisters bandaged blisters in the
neighborhood. It was divine. Old men spun
old stories and dared to spin some
heartbreak, too. We drank their finest lines. It
was divine. Winter's cold came and crept into
the living bones it could find. The people
huddled tight to survive til dawn. It was
divine. When morning broke, the Muezzin's
call rang out like a soulful mist so fine. It was
divine. The people buried who they could
find. It was divine. Between the wailing,
families ate watermelon down to the rind. It
was divine. The last I saw was a rising
Levantine. An entire sun of beauty in full
shine. It was divine.

In a divine relationship, the student inspires and therefore teaches the teacher. The roles become role-less. Spiritual fertilization occurs in both fields of soul. This is also true collectively. When a people suffer profoundly, humanity, to the degree that it is dilated and humble, is washed into a supernatural mutuality of grief and clarity. In this intense froth, souls blend into a union of truth. Delusions fall away. All that is left, the only rope or ladder out of the abyss, is Love. When the intimacy of suffering breaks out across the world, it is vital that we grow still and pay close attention. The sacred teacher and student in us are both being summoned to reckoning. The ceremony cannot begin until we surrender to the lesson.

In a world of enslaved minds, your desire that souls be free from oppression may cause an uproar. From the enslaved. Stay tree-like in your rootedness. Since we have already decided that you are a tree, if you are faltering in the gusts of atrocity, root deeper. Earth yourself.

Those souls violently out of tune with humanity, who know only to destroy humanity, cannot be brought into harmony with humanity by reason, morality, or rationale. They must be stopped. A force more determined than their disease must stop them. Love is such a force. It is not enough to tolerate or have sympathy for a people who are being horribly assaulted. We must Love them, or we will not find the will to struggle with them. The same Love that would have us sacrifice comfort and do anything to protect our own children is required to stop horrific mass violence. If we cannot muster such Love, then it is we who need to purge our socialized poison and heal. Mild hearts cannot for long bear the pressures of revolution. These struggles are for the sacred ferocity of Lovers.

If you wait for an oppressor to change their
mind, you will wait forever. Oppressors have
no mind to change. They do not operate from
reason, but from feverish disease. Do not wait
or explain. Act. Determine to end the horror.

Dear children: Sacred soft soil entrusted with our care. What bedtime stories can we tell you that lessen the terror of the sky predators that fall on you endlessly in the night. That comfort you against the cold, soulless tanks. The fallen walls. The frigid air. The piling rubble. The screams you have not been designed to hear. The limp, lifeless bodies that should be dancing. You are starving. You have not eaten peace in ages. Safety is a ghost you chase across the plains of your nightmares. Come into our arms with your sea of trauma. Spill it out. We pray our hardened hearts can hold it. You are the sweetest, softest soil. We are painfully sorry that far more than seeds have been planted in your earth. We pray for you a springtime. Something wet and warm to turn and clear the ground. And a fresh scent of new things growing that does not feel like empty promises in the sanctuary of your hope.

Acquiescence to the status quo is easy. The struggle of collective freedom is a spiritual odyssey of a lifetime. Here is your mission, should you choose to accept it: Reorder the world order.

Once you realize governments are not gods, politicians are not prophets, and power is in the people, it becomes easier to think and feel for yourself, trust your soul compass, and have faith in the constitution of your compassionate heart.

It is thus. Sometimes you are the well water from which others drink. Sometimes you are the thirst. Sometimes you are the hope fire burning in the horror. Sometimes you are despair on its knees in prayer. We bleed each other. We need each other.

This is grief: Love walks into a wall, bruises
deep, drops off a cliff far too steep, drowns in
the ocean, tosses inside a hurricane, meets an
impossible pain, blisters in the sun, chokes on
fumes, plummets from a cloud, is buried in
cold dirt, burns in an inferno, settles in a
stream, eases up into sky, a dandelion seed,
bleeds and bleeds and bleeds, murmurs,
pauses, claws, panics, breathes, clarifies,
remembers sweetly, shapes a new clay, dares
a new day, holsters agony, rips apart, dares to
start, valleys out, peaks and shouts, is cast
about, turned inside out, denies the truth,
surrenders, holds on dearly, lets go, dreams
the past then wakes to ache, cries a million
lakes, laughs again, grows determined, is
scalded, stripped, simplified, reorganized,
prays for mercy, cannot bear and yet bears it
through, sloshes, boils, calms and callouses,
softens, fades then roars, no end, no end, just
carries on, smiles one day at the beauty of
reaching another dawn, pawns the past,
begrudges the future, goes wide eyed to
realize healing, talks about it, holds it in,
tumbles back and forth, finds a groove,
however shaky, peels off layers, lets it burn,

lets it bake, stays what it is, remains anew.
Love walks into a wall. This is grief.

Some poems you read. Some poems you cry.
Some poems you bleed. Dehumanization and
genocide are all of these.

It is because we Love so deeply that we resist
so passionately the oppressive harm that is
not Love. Our lives are only as beautiful as
they are because so many souls along the
generations sacrificed their comforts and gave
what they could for collective freedom to
grow in our world. Their calling was to reject
empire and conquest and to be courageous
enough for harmonious coexistence. This is
the Beauty Way. It is sacred and worthy of our
freedom fire. This human world is an ocean of
two tides: oppression and freedom. They
swell and rise and pitch against each other,
always. The devotion each of us chooses
inside our soul is and always has been the
force that decides our ocean. You can be
devoted to oppression or to freedom. You
decide us. It was always you.

I am so in Love with trees. They show us how to live and give us everything. If we knew how much they Loved us, we would give them everything.

Let the horrible deepen your
devotion to the heavenly.

I have come from far away to bring you close. You have been freezing all your life, running from the warming fire. Your yearning is nothing compared to the holiness that yearns for you. Others invite you into their home. I invite you into your deepest soul, the home without walls where you may find two treasures you have been seeking: the certainty that you are beautiful and that you belong. For this homecoming to happen, you must give up precious attachment to this way of life that says some groups are worthy of freedom and others deserve to suffer collectively. The peace to which I invite you is going to cost you your supremacies. Are you ready for human power arrangements to die? Are you capable of harmonious coexistence? Can you tolerate dehumanized people being truly free? If you want to ease your suffering, you must reckon with your soul. You can uphold the world you have known, or you can grant passage for what is coming. Behold the glory of soul water rising.

.159.

Another day alive that we get to continue learning how to direct our lives so that all living things are free.

As for human fate, no mass violence is
ultimately about the immediately violated or
the immediate violator. Mass violence is a
revelation of our collective human condition.
Are we bystanders to each other's fate, or do
we dare take accountability for our own role
in the river of relations that brings mass
violence to life and to its end? Who are we,
you and I, not when our life is comfortable
enough but when other lives are desperately
screaming into the abyss? You and I, we
choose each day to buttress or to dismantle
the state of things. In both cases, we work the
clay of human culture. We are never not the
sculptor. But we can be an art that heals. We
can be this.

The freedom of an entire people from systemic oppression is not the same freedom as freedom for individuals to enact harm or to escape accountability for harm. To confuse or conflate these two freedoms is a grave danger and a seed for further systemic oppression. The freedom to exist is not the freedom to oppress. Nor is collective freedom the same truth as personal license. Collective freedom is not a spiteful, vengeful, retributive ego exercise. Collective freedom is a spiritually challenging, persistently woven social condition: transient, mercurial, and in perpetual need of maintenance. When we say, *Freedom for all living things*, we are not saying, *Personal license to do harm*. We are saying, *May all living things exist as both the beneficiaries and safekeepers of collective freedom*. We pray mercy for our imperfection.

You have seen bread rise and moon rise and sun rise. Have you seen a people rise? Behold the irresistible, incandescent human spirit.

The student asked the teacher, *Which should I be doing, Loving or praying?* The teacher answered, *Loving IS praying.*

Our sediment is being stirred. What was at the bottom is coming to the top. Some of it is horrific. Devastating. Diseased. And some of it is an uprising of human beauty against the machine that we have never seen before. Stay close to the beauty. Be its devoted ambassador. Plant redemption seeds.

Rehumanize in your own heart who has been dehumanized in the world. Beautify in your own eyes who has been villainized, demonized, criminalized, and stigmatized by oppressive forces. Monster-making is the step before killing those who have been declared monsters. Monster-making is good business and good empire maintenance. Let no one determine for you who the monsters are. For, the monsters care not at all to abide by group identities. The monsters are freelancers, free agents, mercenaries. As for you, your labor is to retain your own soul.

What fresh poetry of soul do you have to
share with us in your lifetime, in our lifetime,
in this vast amphitheater of coexistence? Let's
you and I root down into our gifts and
see what medicine we can each bring to the
market. The time has come upon us as
humankind to gather in a sacred way. This is
how we will end the horrors and birth our
prayers. Things will happen in this circle that
terrify those who want to conquer
everything. Things will happen in this circle
that delight those who want to conquer
nothing at all. You are more valuable to us
than you know. We hope you attend.

It is not an easy thing to learn to be
collectively free. You have to be willing to let
go of your masters.

We decide what comes next.
Let us decide sacredly.

We spend these words on you who are devoted to this old, dying arrangement. We pour these words toward you who are convicted of malice, who cling to your palace even as it crumbles. We weave these words not for you in your contortion, but for us in our revival. And we say, and we say this: We are not as easy a prey as you may think. We are not a person, nor even a single tribe. Look across earth. We are there. All the places you cannot bear us, we are there, a persistence rising from the roadside, a sweet aura in the trees. We live in breeze. We are all the people of all our people. And we, we are resurgent as sunrise. You can take our lands, our relations, our bread, our bodies, our rains. You cannot take our souls that belong to life's eternity and are woven into the light of stars and the wet of rivers. You can burn our language, but the ashes will form words again and incite revolution. Your harm has made our calligraphy a pool of tears. But still, we shape beautiful stories from the percolation of our passion. We are no nation. We preceded boundaries and borders. We will outlast them all. We have no roofs, but we have roots. We have no water, but we have our oceans of memory. We have ladders out of forgetting. We have ceremony. We have kindness. Our existence is not a tirade of torment and torture. How exhausted you must be to spend your breaths and heartbeats holding us down everywhere on this earth you find us. We spend our breaths breathing, our heartbeats drumming joy. We know how to dance. Our ancestors still whisper to us through the dust of what you have destroyed. We walk as ghosts shrouded in this dust, in this dusk of joy, and yet we are more alive than you, for look at what you have destroyed. Yourselves. For so long. Do you remember feeling Love? Were you afforded this at birth or had the training already begun? Look at what you have done to the sun. Sky is burning with the embers of wailing. Throats have been destroyed. But we, we still have souls. We still feed each other warm soup, even if it is thin and boneless. We still are capable of spotting beauty on the sidewalk and letting our hearts bloom. We are still beautiful. Look at us. Look into our eyes. Souls still swim there. We experience now the loneliness of impossible grief. But we are not as lonely as you. We are not as lonely as you. For your castles have reached their end. How many dishonest mirrors and imaginary walls must you be holding up to explain your centuries of harmfulness. Your fear has consumed you. You have cornered yourself. Your calculus was always doomed. Our tide is rising. Your way is sand. Our tide is typhoon. We are speaking to you the person, not the people. You are not a people. You are lost in conformity's nightmare. Your night does not end. We are not a person. We are all the pain that has ever pained. From this pain we have made prophets. We farm poetry and make families and generations and stories. We make Love. We still feel things besides rage. We still grow deep things and pulse with sweet things and dream of beauty for our neighbors. We are not obsessed with taking. We are pregnant with giving. We still celebrate in the river. Our hearts are dilated to life, not to destruction's draft. We do not expire. We make Love. Do not rush away from what you are doing. Witness yourself. And now, please excuse us. We are still in Love, and so now we pray. We swim with God. We cry mercy. Pay close attention to how we die. It will teach you something about how we live.

But what does it mean to break free? To express the altitude of our soul desire and sink down into the root and flow out into the river, and become breeze, and become power, become memory. What does it mean to wander the desert for forty tears. What does it mean to bring back the bark of the tree. To release the butterflies to the sky. To become canopy. To vibrate and earthquake our fate, our reach, our desire, yearning, burning, spinning, giving. What does it mean to be a living thing. To fight, to flounder, to fall, to fail, to fade, to rise again into the mortal mist. Breathe. Breathe. Breathe. Breathe.

.173.

Only when humans finally come to believe
that pure, holy, divine Love is a more
powerful force than the terrified bravado that
is hate, will we activate our fullest capacity
and creativity to grow a way of life in which
harmonious coexistence is the steadfast rule
of life.

The nature of a parasite is such that it can remain in a body indefinitely as long as it does not overburden the body. A kind of sick symbiosis. But when the parasite becomes desperate and wreaks more havoc within the body, the body's immune system ramps up in urgency and does all that it can to expel the parasite. This too is so with oppressive supremacy systems. When such a parasite grows desperate and begins killing everything and everyone with a blatancy, the collective body human at last finds the urgency to peak its spiritual immune system and expel the pathology. The binding forces of kinship rally against the acute and chronic sickness and purge the pathology. And here we are.

Your body is designed for revolution. It rises
up against and expels what is diseased and
pathological. If your body can defend itself
against harm and act for its own well-being,
you can too for humanity. You are designed to
be an active agent in defense and promotion
of the collective human body. You are
medicine. Flow to what needs healing.

It is never a bad time to revolt
against systems of harm.

If you understood that your heart is the heart
of all of Creation pulsing in you, you would
have more faith in the power of your Love.

When you are in crisis, see who shows up for you. Much will be revealed. When an entire people are in crisis, see how you show up for them. Much will be revealed.

Gather with your kindred spirits. Weave with
them a fabric of prayers. Let the birth waters
come. Talk story that gives life. Paint your
totems bright. Sing your rebellions. Ask your
pain to show you the path. Rest like a lion.
Wake like sunrise. Let the babies suckle in the
circle. Ask the harmful old ways to leave.
Invite Glory. Do not limit the guests it brings.
You have dreams. They wait dancing for you
to grant them land. A bee lands on you,
thinking you to be a flower. Maybe you have
been petals and pollen all along.

.180.

We can say that mobilizing against destructive systems is exhausting. And yet, each revolutionary breath moves us closer to a way of life in which souls are able to rest deeper and live more fruitfully than they ever have.

Why should you care about the suffering of others? *Your life*. What should you offer? *Your life*. What of yours will benefit? *Your life*. For how long should you serve? *Your life*.

Find in your soul your truest Love song and
sing it with all your life, as though this world
depends on it. For it does.

BeLoved. Over the course of your life, you have built a fortress of stories to protect yourself. This fortress may now be a prison keeping you from dissolving into the Great Beauty of life, a profound oneness of being that fulfills your purpose and harbors only harmony among living things. Humanity needs you now. Yes, it does. You have reached your moment. Lose your fortress. Serve this Calling. Dissolve and join the Everything.

Truth can be an arrow that penetrates collective denial. If you are a Lover who wants revolution, do not hesitate to pull and release the bow. Collective denial requires mass cooperation. An agreement not to face things as they are, to pretend that hell is heaven. Systems of oppression depend on these agreements. When you disagree and resist conforming, you loosen your precious personal thread from the fabric of harm. You, through your contagious refusal, can unspool the madness and birth sacredness from the womb of your uprising. The long night of oppression seems inevitable. Until you light the candle that is your uncolonized soul.

Because you exist, you have the power to feed the status quo or to starve it. Some things are rabid and need to expire.

Be a curator of the beauty that lives in the
souls of those in harm's way. This is how you
remain human. Hold their beauty in your
heart. Holding beauty sparks freedom fires.

If a soul moves you, let them know. We can
move beyond transactional, predatory
compliment culture out into the bright
healing fields where we nurture each other by
simply saying, You move me. As we grow this
sacred way together, we fill the collective
gourd of affirmation, kinship, worth, Love,
and belonging. This is our supply route to
freedom.

The truth always tells on itself, no matter who is hiding it. Collective freedom is a nudist forever shedding its oppression clothes.

It is time to lay to rest the lie that you are
small and helpless against the apparent might
of monsters. Drink now this elixir of truth: You
are might, mountain, majesty, miracle,
medicine, moon, ministry, mission, marvel,
mayhem. You are more than sufficient to
overturn false empires. Do not bathe in fear.
It will drown you. Bathe in your power. It will
give you life.

The roots of mass harm are mass indifference.
The human will to protect what we care
about is infinite and eternal. May we break
free from our prejudices so that our Love
floods into those spaces in the soul that allow
us to care about all of this Creation. The
truest poetry of your life can be found in how
you respond to oppressive harm. These are
your purest verses. They drip with rebellion
and sing like paradise.

If you are alive at this time on earth, you have
a role to play. You are not in the audience.
You are on stage. You have already been cued
to action. Your lines are redemption songs.

Have you noticed the whisper roaming this world? The trees are telling us it is time for oppressive systems to die.

We must look evil straight in the eye, or we
will never recognize that it has no soul. Upon
seeing this vacancy, we will act accordingly.
We are gardeners of the next world,
preparing the soil. Where there are predatory
threats in the ground where we plant
freedom, we shall cast them away. The future,
too, is a sacred land. We are its stewards. And
so, we rise up and do our earthing duty.

All empires, in that they are necessarily
oppressive, are collective suffering souls.
Their violence is not a reflection
of their right to exist but of the burden of
their unnatural existence. They cannot help
themselves. They explode outward because
they implode with desperation. They are
forever haunted, vexed, marked, doomed. It is
a deep mercy, BeLoved, for you to do all that
you can to end their unnatural tyranny. We
are going to need so much more grace and
mercy.

The longer a particular mass violence exists,
the more humans tend to accept it as normal
and inevitable. Resisting the seeping
saturation of personal acceptance of mass
harm is the spiritual heart of a revolution.
Who are the firekeepers who stay away the
cold of our numbness? Help them gather the
firewood.

Suffering knows no borders. This is why our hearts must be borderless, too. When you birth from soul and spirit as opposed to from ego, what you birth is timeless because soul and spirit are eternal and beyond time. Does your heart feel not big enough for all this violence, pain, and grief? Use your collective heart. It is always with you, and always big enough. Your collective heart is the ancestral deep water where revolution surges, crests, and rests. As for your compassion. You may believe that you have been occupying your whole heart. You have been swimming in a puddle, a tidepool on the shores of your heart. Your heart is an ocean. So much more Love lives in you.

BeLoved. Do you see how desperate the
controlling, hoarding class is for you to
continue participating in their violent,
devastating, generational game of monopoly?
Do not confuse their fear and anger for
justified passion. Your enslavement is their
life raft, and the ocean of their delusion is
swallowing them. The flames of our
revolution are growing. Oh, the Glory of our
soul arousal. Ancestors are circling us now. A
glint is gaining in their eyes.

Our grief is an ocean of tears so hot that they have melted into one another. Only Love can swim this scalding sorrow-water and reach the shore of collective human healing. Only Love activated into a cause that refuses to wilt over time and generations. Only a Love so doused in determination that its roar pierces the chrysalis and calyx of the galaxy and lets in new light and fresh wings. Only a ferocious ancestral wail can break us free. We can no longer afford to grieve timid, alone, and despairing. We must grieve bravely, boldly, and gathered in spiritual revival. We need the old songs. We need hailstorms of rebellion. We need a record harvest. We need unbrokered, feral birth waters and delirious midwives who cannot bear the norm. We need you. Absolutely shed and shorn from your lifelong conditioning. We need you rampant and raw and lustful for freedom, standing in the center of this uncountable graveyard and braying at the sky for sanctity to pour out over each fallen, risen soul. We need you to be you in ways you have never managed to be you. We need you epiphanied and portaled and pilloried by Love's courage-dipped arrows. We need you as old as the

.199.

oldest trees, pocked deep as moon, and
absurd like a jungle. Yes, we need you lush
and lifelike and supernaturally alive.

A mountain cannot pass through an
hourglass. But sand can. Your unbroken heart
cannot pass through grief. But your broken
heart can. Love cannot breach you hard and
proud and coiled. But if you are crumbled and
humbled, Love can make of you a miraculous
medicine for this world. Let yourself feel what
there is to feel. Let yourself be broken.

May you take the opportunity that this
moment on earth provides to practice
discerning between those voices that want to
exploit humanity and those voices that want
to heal humanity. Both are convinced. Don't
let both be convincing.

Something about acting on behalf of others in harm's way. It removes harm from our own way. Imagine that. Kindred care.

To say it is hypocritical to live inside an
oppressive system while critiquing and
dismantling it is like saying it is hypocritical to
breathe air while you are trying to clean it.

So many worlds live inside you that you have
yet to bless with the vast sunlight of your
attention. In some of those worlds, violence
and oppression are treated with appropriate
response and a humanizing kindness grazes
freely. If you yearn for such worlds to become
more prominent in your being, you are going
to have to spend time on those planets. They
need you to be their constant sun.

When an elephant senses its death, it may separate itself from the herd and change to light in solitude. Your healing and growth require many deaths, and therefore many Loving solitudes. May you not be afraid of being with your own soul when it calls for you. All of life lives within your aloneness, too.

Do not gaze upon the human condition as
though you are apart from that condition.
Gaze as though you are a mother gazing her
infant. Then, see how you are moved to act.
Nothing at all is happening in this world that
is not also happening to you. May we
caretake each other accordingly. Now you see
that your inner condition is a strand in the
web of our collective condition. If you can
become a whole new world, so can we. So
can we.

The child you once were would look up at the
person you are now with eyes wide and in
awe. I hope you remember this when you
need to.

The thing about sacred land, whether the
earth, a people, humanity, or your body,
calling, dreams, or the future, is that you
must be willing to honor and protect your
sacred land. Hungry ghosts will come for it.
You must not run from them, or worse,
silence yourself in fear of public sanctioning.
You are the steward and caretaker of your
sacred land. You must use all manner of
ceremony to protect its sovereignty and
resurrect its vitality after harm. Your sacred
land needs you wild and ablaze with passion.
It needs you ignited into creative, resourceful,
determined resistance, joy, and beauty. Let's
say you are a dancer. Your sacred land needs
the festive, feasting, faithful fury of your feet.

When we hurt, two paths emerge in our heart. One path deepens our hurt. The other path begins to heal our hurt. The difference between these two paths is the story we tell ourselves about the meaning of our hurt. This storytelling also shapes how we respond when an entire group of people are being harmed horrifically. Hurt is a messenger. It is also a mystic doorway opening to who we choose to be.

When you are truly secure in the divine
beauty of your own existence, acting ugly is a
far less tempting path to take. Have you read
the Gospel of your own soul? The people,
scriptures, and parables there may heal and
set you free.

When evil erupts, the human must ask
humanity and humanity must ask the human,
Where is your soul?

Humanity is suffering for many reasons. One is that in our always accelerating inner and outer condition, we have abandoned the realm of miracle. Life is a menagerie of subtle and sensational miracles. To be truly immersed in miracle, to see, feel, and be moved by miracle, requires stillness, presence, intention, and attention. All of which we lose by rushing anxiously through moments that could have offered us their miracles. Instead, we experience the madness of chronic malaise. Experiencing a miracle is a blessing. Recognizing the miracles that you are experiencing blesses the blessing. You and I are designed to live in a condition of miraculousness. Of divine, purposeful, interwoven wonder. If we are going to heal our devastating, destructive impulses, we must remember our miracle nature and the miracle nature all around us. We have long been vagrant. It is time to come home to our holy design.

All living things are given the capacity to
protect the well-being of their kind. Who is
your kind? A fatal question. You, dear soul,
have been given the divine instrument that is
Love. Care for your instrument. Use it
bountifully.

Evil does not change its mind. Like a virus, it continues to grow, spread, and do harm as long as it is unchecked. Your Love for other people's freedom is the only force that can stop oppressive devastation. You must be the protective, pure-hearted, fierce lily of the valley. Hone your Holy Love.

Many people believe they would recognize genocide when it happens and would take moral action. After genocide, many create stories to absolve themselves from the truth that genocide happened, and they chose not to see or to act. Humans and human cultures are composed of stories. Stories seed, gestate, birth, protect, and raise genocide. Stories can end genocide, too. Heal your stories. Did you rinse it off before you ate it? Your cultural conditioning, that is.

When you look with Sacred eyes upon this world, you see that all healthy living things are giving their lives for freedom of the whole. They can see and feel the whole move through them, a constant river, and they know that the destiny of the whole is their destiny, too. You may despair that humankind has never been without hateful oppression. Our ancestors say to us, *Remember: Humankind has never been without resistance to oppression. We are never without Love's insistent Glory. Remember.*

When we gather in Love and fierce
determination for collective freedom, we
summon the power of life itself, which no
malice can run asunder. This, BeLoved, is our
medicine. Caring for the freedom of others
blesses your generations. Do you see how sun
and moon are with each other? They are
teaching us that powerful things can coexist
in harmony.

It is not that we have so much to learn. It is that we have so much to remember. We are alive in the colonizing centuries of the Great Forgetting. Let us journey now into this new era upon us of the Great Remembering. We need teachers gifted not at cold instruction but at Loving reunion. We need homecoming.

Oppression is pathetic and obsolete.
May we stop worshipping empires.

Do not let anyone tell you
that freedom is complicated.

Hafez, Saadi, Rumi, Attar, Sanai, Khayyam, and all the Persian mystic poets walk with me. We are the interwoven roots of the same poet tree. Their mist is my breath. Their heartbeat my pulse. We are the same blood river, a spirit that has tasted all the ages and savored them. In the spirit world, we sit around the fire and laugh and cry stories until the bloom of dawn. I came into this world as a scroll imprinted with their dewy Love letters. All my life I have been weeping the words. The gift is not my writing. The gift is the light of God in my soul that illuminates the words. Creator is the author. I am the imperfect scribe. With words, I work in the cotton, corn, cane fields of sacred prayer. Open your heart. Meet me there. I am a poor, passionate student. My countless teachers have taught me this: Life's irrepressible ocean does not care about our stubborn biases and prideful hostilities. This Great Water just wants to drown us in its essence. Which, of course, is Love.

When a child is sick, the parent who responds
with immediacy and care is praised as Loving
and devoted. When humanity is sick, those
who respond with immediacy and care are
scorned and mocked by worshippers of the
status quo. You are not here to please those
addicted to the norm. You are a sacred
steward. A caretaker. Honor your devotion.

Love is the most demanding law of all. It does not tolerate any excuses for oppressive behavior. There is that which is Love and that which is not Love. Both have their massive fate. This world is not your garbage dump, object to possess, or punching bag for your violence. This world is a garden, and your assignment is to be its gardener. No greater priority exists than that you care for this glorious gift. All of it. Sickness in souls pushes our humanity toward destruction. Be the medicine that returns us home to Love's sanctuary. Actual Love will cost you all your ideas of Love. Where there is oppressive harm, Love dives in.

.224.

Because we are Lovers, we resist forever what
is not Love. Because we are Lovers, we face
the truth and bloom. Because we are Lovers,
we care for the collective wound. Because we
are Lovers, we pour medicine, not malice.
Because we are Lovers, we stay in the fire. We
burn and burn with remembering.

In the garden of your true heart, you act
decisively against oppressive harm. All that is
left is to bring your action out into the world,
which, too, is a garden. Freedom is not kin to
self-concern. It is the offspring of caring for
the whole thing. The *wholespring*. Do you
want a tomorrow? Be brave against tyranny
today. Oppressive partnerships worldwide are
descending further into madness and
desperation. Root yourself in the people
of the lands. Ascend further into revolution.
Caste systems don't end themselves. They
reveal themselves. The people must end
them. But first, the people must believe the
revelation.

Culture can raise you into a beautiful living thing and culture can raze you into a soulless monster. Take great care with what you let shape you. This world depends on your discernment.

Young people are the candlelight of revolution. And its roar. Every mass movement against oppression and apartheid has been ignited and sustained by young people and students. Our young still taste heaven in their hearts and they want more of it on earth. They have not yet surrendered to the chains of dehumanization. They choke on the pathology and poison. They dare mount freedom.

Many things are being exhumed, erased, silenced, revealed. All that is left is for human decency to overcome human addiction to systems of greed, violence, and suffering.

One day, they will come for you and yours.
What happens then will be the ripple from
what you and I do or do not do today. Life's
favorite poetry is when you choose to stand
and act for collective freedom.

One day, it will be clear that humanity was in this time rejecting not one group or nation, but the entire world of exploitation and its centuries of harm. Resisting the disease of dehumanization is a sacred act. What Glory to join the chorus of living things choosing sacred coexistence over violence, greed, and control.

Institutions will enable the worst oppressive
violence before they ever tolerate internal
disorder. They would rather brutalize their
own people than stand against brutality in
which they are complicit and culpable. They
will kill their young before they divest from
the killing of other young. Internal order is
their god, and their value of justice is a fraud
revealed when humanity finally surges against
the forces that made such institutions
wealthy and revered in the first place. We live
now in a time when institutions reveal their
true gods. Revolution reveals that the people
and only the people can be trusted to uphold
morality. The people, the pueblo, are where
Love and its freedom grows. Behold.
Revolution is a revealer of gods.

Love is the life force that heals.
Any true revolution is Love.

Some people have neither the capacity nor the desire to be there for you when you are moving through a hard moment. They only want your light. Those who show up without condition and genuinely care for you, not only the glory of you, are worthy of your presence. Share your essence with those whose interest in you is more than a mood. They will stay with you through the fire. Until the garden after.

A flame of Love for all living things burns in your heart. This flame can be doused by a lifetime of dehumanizing ideas about others. Do not let this flame go out. If this flame goes out, your soul goes out. Your duty is to be the sacred firekeeper of your own compassionate heart.

How many flowers must die before we consider the garden sick and set about healing it? We cannot achieve collective healing without reckoning with the roots of our collective suffering. Today's horror is not a new thing. It is an old thing erupted anew. History wears fresh clothes, and we think it a stranger. This dehumanization disease is very, very old. Let us put it out of its misery and be creative in what we choose to birth. Another day that you and I are alive to work for collective freedom. What a gift to be able to grow as an ancestor. Joy in your heart and freedom in the world are intimate kin.

No revolution for social justice and collective freedom has enjoyed initial overwhelming support. Many humans cling to what they know even if what they know is devastation and misery. To birth a new way, we must overcome deeply rooted social norms and identity attachments. Status quo is a worshipped god within the heart of fear. The mountain a revolution must scale is not only a mountain of ideas but also the acutely possessive mountain of the familiar.

May you be so very gentle with yourself.
Even now, you are just beginning. You are not
feeling only yourself. You are feeling the
world. You have oceans of feeling to care for.
Be present in this. Your heart, with every
beat, sends you a Love letter called Life. You
in your living can be a heartbeat for those
under the assault of oppression. Be enduring
as you pulse out into this world the action
blood of your devotion to collective freedom.

At this time on earth, we are deciding
whether this human era is the last human era.
Or the beginning of unprecedented healing.
The transition that will determine humanity is
the spiritual shift from, *They are being killed*,
to, *We are being killed*, and, *We are killing*.
The rise of the *We* will set us free. Bless you,
for you are alive on earth in an era of
profound, historical reckoning. This era is for
truth telling, truth dwelling, and truth
rebelling. You may believe that your pain is a
separate pain from the world's pain. When
you unlearn this, your deepest healing may
begin. You are a strand in the sacred web of
life. Your duty is to be relational. To care.
Writing Love letters is beautiful. Being a Love
letter is divine. May you be a Love letter to
this world today.

Warriors are not hard as stone. Warriors are soft as soil, song, petals, prayer, womb, water. Warriors weep. May you not let this world convince you that your tenderness needs repairing. Your deep feeling heart too is a pollinator. And here is a prayer that we create together a world that allows souls to enjoy the blessings of a regulated, tranquil nervous system. A healing nervous system is one of the most meaningful, fruitful gifts you can offer your relationships and the world. And, although it may challenge us, may we be devoted to not yelling and screaming at our children. It harms their nervous systems for life. We should know. We are still healing. Please take wonderful care of your precious heart. Our collective future is growing in that sacred garden. Can you feel it all in the world in this moment? The turning? Be so very gentle. Tender needs tenderness. And tender rest. Life is a perpetual womb and each of us is in an endless birth. Go easy. We need you well enough for revolution.

If your art comes from the sacred storm and serenity that is Love, worry not, for it is the very marrow of revolution. Does your art simmer with the integrity of truth as you birth it? Then your art is most worthy of a liberated humanity. You are a storyteller of what this world is. Your ideas, beliefs, prejudices, inherited understandings, affinities, aversions, soul persona, pain, Love, inner condition, and intentions determine what, through countless mediums, you say to yourself and to the world. You beget other storytellers. Be willing to examine what has shaped your fateful *Word*. This is not trivial. This is collective salvation. Be very careful who you let be your storyteller as you behold a revolution. And know this: People will tell stories about you. Your life will be determined by the stories you tell about you, *to you*.

A fundamental and fatal human
miscalculation is that we were ever safe, are
safe, will be safe if we just do nothing when
others are in harm's way. The cause of their
harm can smell the scent of our apathy and is
relentlessly paving a road directly to the
convenient heart of our inaction and
disregard. The delusion that we are safe calls
in all predators.

If you do not know the story of a people's soul beauty, you can be easy prey for those who want you to accept harm to those people. Keep your compassion deeper than your group identities. Invest yourself in learning humanity beyond your own humanity. Be a connoisseur of soul beauty. Living things turn toward Sun as it rises. So should our hearts turn toward a people as they rise into freedom. Liberation never savors just one group of people. Liberation of any people is a freedom reservoir for all people. When chains are broken, all living things can feel them fall.

No way around it. Your heart is going to
break. You may as well let it break into
freedom. Not just yours. Theirs. Ours.
All things. Freedom is not a breakdown. It is a
breakout. In a sick world it takes a kind of
fever to break free. May you never approach
that doomscape abyss in whose horrid
purgatory the slaughter of masses makes
sense to you. May you remain a kind of flower
in league with beauty. I pray your soul acres
are receiving good rain and sun, and beautiful
things are arriving, sprouting, lifting,
blooming, fruiting. You are so beautiful a
tattoo on this ardent earth.

When it comes to doing what you can to end
mass, oppressive suffering, you are not just
the drinker of the freedom tea. You are the
fire that boils the water. Believe in the power
of your compassion flame. Do not leave
behind in the endless trash bins of conformity
your precious empathy. It is your salvation.
And ours. Reject the lie that your compassion
is a weakness. Through your empathic caring,
you water the human garden. In this season
of horrific drought, we could use your
monsoon. The mystery for you to solve is not:
How can you save humanity? The mystery for
you to solve is: How can you dissolve the
prejudice, fear, and paralysis in you that
obstruct Love from flowing freely through
you? How can you unleash Love's monsoon?
When you liberate Love within you, Love
leaps forth from you as a sacred action
powerful enough to overcome our human
horrors. When you free your Love Prophet,
Greatness reigns. Love's rapture saves
humanity.

Do not let oppressors fatigue you. Fatigue those who oppress. Be stubborn with your freedom vows. When a blight plagues the world, do not be the bystander. Be the medicine. Be the fire. And as you get older, dream not weaker, dream bolder. Be a wildfire. Don't smolder. What a volcano does when it's fed up. Freedom like that.

How to prepare for war: Do not prepare for war. Prepare for Love. Then you will be prepared for war. And life. And life.

The wild choreography of living things
growing and healing together according to
the laws of symbiosis and mutually beneficial
kinship. Let this be our holy freedom anthem.
When humanity learns to hold genuine,
sincere, devoted care as the heart of all our
relations, work, creativity, and healing, we will
begin to taste the divine sunrise of freedom.

She had wed many things in her life. But never peace. It would be the greatest matrimony of her lifetime. She gathered her soul's harvest of courage and faith and prepared for all of us a feast of healing and harmony. Her generations, and yours and mine, forever drank the blessing. Our sleep was divine. Our lives hummed a new song whose notes dripped honey and heaven. It was good. Oh, it was good.

You will need to say goodbye to many
impostors inside you to arrive at who you
truly are. A lifetime of performance and
pleasing has left you crowded with a cast of
false selves. Your long show is over. Now your
life is a ceremony of truth. Prepare to feast on
a peace you have never known. For some,
peace visits from time to time. Hold fast to
your healing, for one day you will say, *Peace
lives in my soul.*

I pray your heart and soul walk in lush
gardens of grace as you round this new sun. I
pray the pomegranates you pluck from the
trees teach you what it means to gather
sweetness, and how to burst with joy when
life takes you in its ravenous mouth. I pray
you free your tears to become baptismal
rivers. You could use a good washing away. I
pray peace will be your close prophet,
whispering to you of how new your life can
be. I pray your heart drum plays a song of
surrender. And that your soul feels the beat
and starts an endless fever dance that feels
like the sweetest water song your generations
have known.

Every living thing has medicine to heal this world. Are you not a living thing? There is a temple in your soul where justice does not waiver. See how much of your life you can spend there, gathering your courage to do what Love would do. Here is the question: Do you want freedom only for you and yours? Or do you want freedom for humanity? Have you come here to be liked, or have you come here to be Life? These are two vastly different paths, dear soul. Deep in your soul, you know the difference between oppression and freedom. Don't wait for the crowd to tell you which one to stand for. Devote yourself.

All living things are a doorway out into truth. Dear soul, how often do you leave the house? Do not mistake or misplace your sacred source. When you live from your soul, you carve the world in prayer. In our world, there is that which breaks things apart and that which brings things together. We must know when to break and when to bind. In each moment, we are malice or medicine. We get to choose. Love does not turn away from the truth of horrible things. What a rose does with sunrise. Do that with your one miraculous life. May your heart sip a thousand cups of peace.

When Harriet Tubman said, *We cross at dark*, she was speaking into the timeless ancestral realm. She was speaking to you. Here we are at the river, my kin. Night is a deeper kind of dark. The river is loud and racing. Now is not the time for you to hope that the future will somehow solve our pain. Now is when the blackbirds blacken the black of our midnight, their wing song urging us to remember why we are here. You have a massive archive of ancestors in you, pouring you their wisdom stew. Do not say you do not have answers. Say you have no more time. We cross now. Freedom is for the fearful, too. Worry not about your tremble. There is no shame in your doubt. Morning Loves you. You are its personal sun. My dear family, we rise now. With us, we bring a most spectacular dawn.

If this book touched you, you can touch it back.

Please kindly consider writing an **online reader review** at various booksellers. Reviews are a valuable way to support the life of a book and especially an independent author.

Freely **post social media photos** of the book, passages from the book, or readings of the book. Please kindly include the hashtag **#jaiyajohn.**

I deeply cherish your support of my medicine words and our Soul Water Rising rehumanizing mission around the world.

BOOK ANGEL PROJECT

Your book purchases support our global *Book Angel Project,* which provides grants and book donations for vulnerable youth, and places gift copies of my *medicine books* throughout pueblos and communities worldwide, to be discovered by the souls who need them. These books are left where hearts are tender: hospitals, nursing homes, prisons, wellness centers, group homes, mental health clinics, and other community spaces.

If you are fortunate to discover one of our *Book Angel* gift books, please kindly post a photo of you with the book on Instagram, using the hashtag **#jaiyajohn,** or email us at **jaiya@soulwater.org**. Thank you much.

I Will Read for You:
The Voice and Writings of Jaiya John

A podcast. Voice medicine to soothe your soul, from poet, author, and spoken word artist Jaiya John. Bedtime bliss. Morning meditation. Daytime peace. Comfort. Calm. Soul food. Come, gather around the fire. Let me read for you. **Spotify. Apple. Wherever podcasts roam.**

Sacred Word with Jaiya John on Substack

Subscribe for free or as a paid supporter to join Jaiya's Sacred Word journal space where he shares his stories, poetry, essays, new book previews, book excerpts, audio and video gifts, product discounts, and guidance on your freedom work, creative life, and sacred healing.

jaiyajohn.com

Dr. Jaiya John was orphan-born on Ancient Puebloan lands in the high desert of New Mexico, and is an internationally recognized freedom worker, poet, author, teacher, and speaker. Jaiya is the founder of Soul Water Rising, a global *rehumanizing* mission to eradicate oppression. The mission has donated thousands of Jaiya's books in support of social healing and offers grants to displaced and vulnerable youth. He is the author of numerous books, including *Daughter Drink This Water, We Birth Freedom at Dawn, Fragrance After Rain*, and *Freedom: Medicine Words for your Brave Revolution*. Jaiya writes, narrates, and produces the podcast, *I Will Read for You: The Voice and Writings of Jaiya John,* and is the founder of *The Gathering*, a global initiative and tour reviving traditional gathering and storytelling practices to fertilize social healing and liberation. He is a former professor of social psychology at Howard University and has spoken to over a million people worldwide and audiences as large as several thousand. Jaiya holds doctorate and master's degrees in social psychology from the University of California, Santa Cruz, with a focus on intergroup and race relations. As an undergraduate, he attended Lewis & Clark College in Portland, Oregon, and lived in Kathmandu, Nepal, where he studied Tibetan Holistic Medicine through independent research with Tibetan doctors and trekked to the base camp of Mt. Everest. His Indigenous soul dreams of frybread, sweetgrass, bamboo in the breeze, and turtle lakes whose poetry is peace.

Learn more at: JAIYAJOHN.COM.

Jacqueline V. Carter served graciously, faithfully, and skillfully as the editor for this book. I am forever grateful for her Love labor.

**Secure a Dr. Jaiya John keynote,
talk, or book reading:**

jaiyajohn.com

OTHER BOOKS BY JAIYA JOHN

Jaiya John titles are available directly at his website, and online worldwide where books are sold. To learn more about this and other books by Jaiya John, to order discounted wholesale quantities, or to learn about Soul Water Rising's global freedom work, please visit us at:

jaiyajohn.com

books@soulwater.org

@jaiyajohn (IG and YT)

www.ingramcontent.com/pod-product-compliance
Lightning Source LLC
Chambersburg PA
CBHW030430160726
47991CB00005B/1675